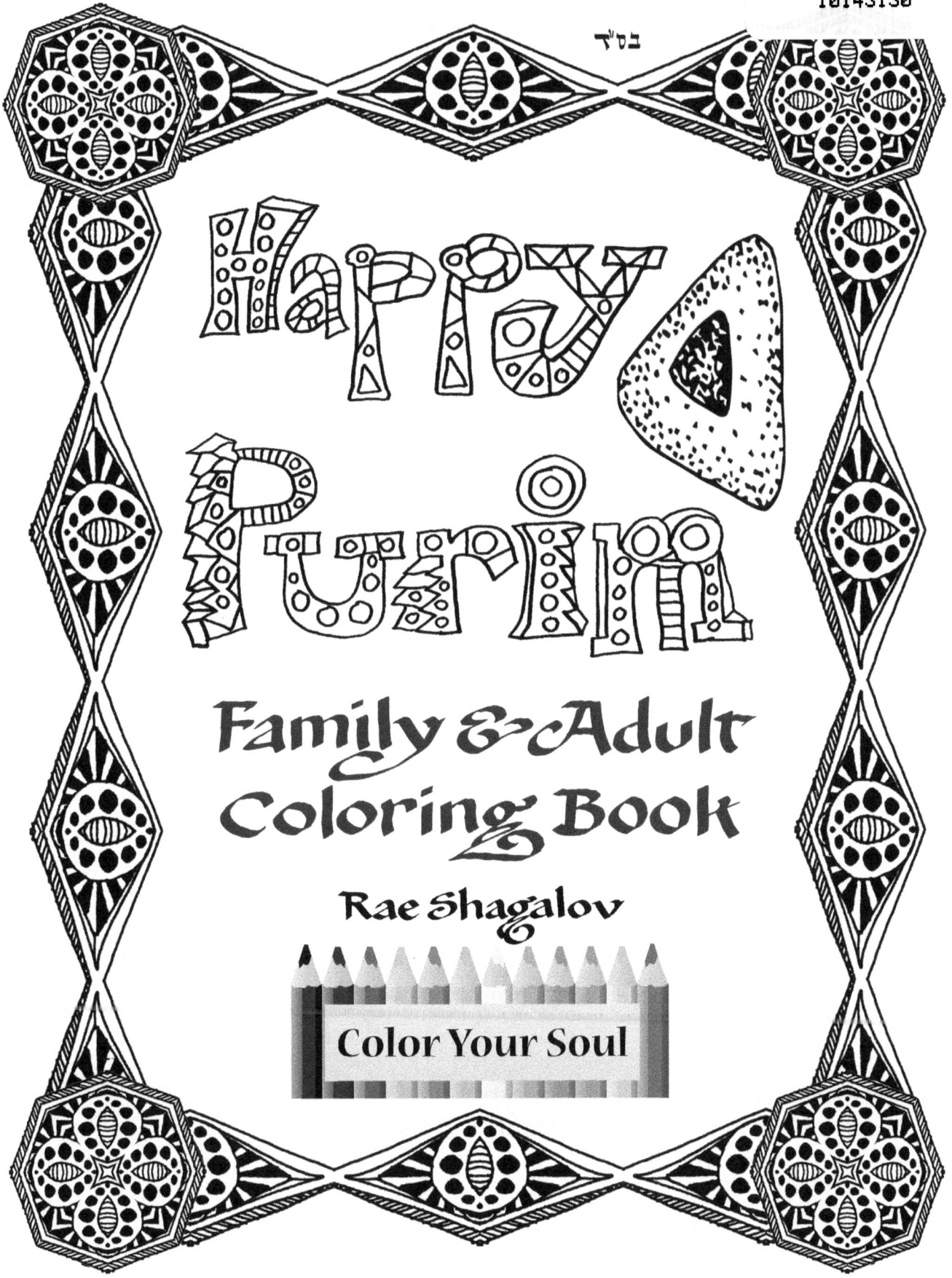

בס״ד

Happy Purim

Family & Adult Coloring Book

Rae Shagalov

Color Your Soul

Printed in the United States of America
First Printing, 2019
ISBN: 978-1-937472-05-4 paperback

Holy Sparks Press
www.holysparks.com
www.joyfullyjewish.com

Los Angeles
Purim Katon 5779
Year of Geulah Gathering

Let's Connect!

Facebook.com/soultips

Pinterest.com/holysparks

Youtube.com/holysparksbooks

Instagram.com/holysparks

Please do not color on Shabbat or Jewish holy days,
as writing and coloring are prohibited by Jewish law
on those days.

This Publication Is Dedicated To The Rebbe,
Rabbi Menachem M. Schneerson of Lubavitch

whose teachings and inspiration lives in us, and fires us up
to try and reach heights we can't reach on our own,
to prepare the whole world for the imminent arrival of Moshiach.

IN LOVING MEMORY OF

Harav Schneur Zalman Halevi ע"ה
ben Harav Yitzchok Elchonon Halevi הי"ד Shagalov

Reb Dovid Asniel ben Reb Eliyahu ע"ה

Devora Rivka bas Reb Yosef Eliezer ע"ה

Reb Yitzchok Moshe ben Reb Dovid Asniel ע"ה

؈   May Their Souls Merit Eternal Life   ؆

AND IN HONOR OF

Mrs. Esther Shaindel bas Fraidel Chedva שתחי' Shagalov
and Our Dear Children and Grandchildren שיחיו
May You Always Be Joyfully Jewish!

DEDICATED BY

Rabbi & Mrs. Yosef Yitzchok and Gittel Rachel שיחיו Shagalov

To dedicate future editions in
honor or memory of your
loved ones, contact us at:
info@holysparks.com

∾ Introduction ∾

I love to learn the secrets of the Torah, about the spiritual energies of our soul, and about all of the ways we can transform this world, little-by-little, into a dwelling place for *G-d. Over the last 25 years, with the help of G-d, I've written 3,000 pages of calligraphy Artnotes, illustrated with graphics suitable for coloring, that record the Jewish wisdom of hundreds of Torah leaders for our special time, the threshold of the Messianic Era of peace.

""Happy Purim" is the second book in the "Color Your Soul" series of family and adult coloring books that integrate the relaxing, meditative art of coloring with deep Chassidic secrets of Judaism. It includes fun designs to color and unique Jewish quotes from contemporary Jewish masters written in beautiful calligraphy. There are labels in various sizes that you can customize and use for your **shalach manos, and any page can enhance your Purim gifts, rolled up as a scroll and tied with a ribbon.

Coloring is a very relaxing, peaceful, meditative activity. As you color in the pages, contemplate the Artnotes thoughts on them and try to internalize them. If you're doing this as a family activity, discuss the ideas while you color them in together. Afterwards, hang up these beautiful family treasures around your home to set a Happy Purim tone.

I would love to see your colorful creations, so let's connect!

Feel free to email me with questions, suggestions & pictures of your coloring at: info@holysparks.com or share them with me on Facebook at: www.facebook.com/soultips

---

*Out of reverence for G-d, the Jewish people often do not spell out the whole name of G-d.

**Shalach Monos are the special gifts of food that we give to the poor and to friends on Purim. For more information about the special mitzvahs of Purim, go to: http://www.chabad.org/holidays/purim

---

*Mitzvahs are Divine Commandments that connect us to G-d.

**Moshiach is the Jewish world leader, a descendent of King David, who will rebuild the Temple in Jerusalem and gather the Jewish people out of exile, back to Israel. Moshiach will lead us into Geulah, a world of complete peace and abundance, without war or suffering. The coming of Moshiach will complete Gd's purpose in creation - for us to make a dwelling place for Gd in this world by transforming and elevating the material things of this world into spirituality through learning Torah and doing mitzvahs and acts of goodness and kindness.

∾ How To Use This Book ∾

Print out on good quality paper and place a piece of cardboard or a few sheets of paper under the page if you are using pens or paints, so the ink won't bleed through. If you are making Purim cards, print out on card stock. If you are making posters for your walls, or scrolls to give as gifts, print out on regular or parchment-type paper.

Gather your colored pencils, pens or paints. Flip through the book and choose a page that sparks your interest. Intuitively choose your colors and don't fret if you make a "mistake" or color outside the lines. Just relax and continue, letting your mind wander and enjoy the colors. Being in this relaxed state will improve your life and outlook, but you can also use it to go higher into holiness.

How? You could listen to a Torah class about Purim while coloring, or you could meditate on the greatness of G-d. When you are in this relaxed state, it is a very good time to think about and speak to G-d about everything you need! It's a wonderful place to be in to think about your life, your family and friends and how you can improve yourself and your relationships. It's a lovely interlude for creatively thinking about a new *mitzvah you would like to do, or imagining how you could do a mitzvah more beautifully than ever before. It's a special time to dream about what the world will be like when **Moshiach comes, G-d willing, very, very soon to usher in the great era of peace that we all wait and wish for. When you do this, you elevate the act of coloring by serving G-d with it.

Rae Shagalov

May G-d keep you from all manner of harm and distress and bless the works of your hands with success, in good health, with great joy, and abundant livelihood – and may you always be Joyfully Jewish!

---

*Mitzvahs are Divine Commandments that connect us to G-d.

**Moshiach is the Jewish world leader, a descendent of King David, who will rebuild the Temple in Jerusalem and gather the Jewish people out of exile, back to Israel. Moshiach will lead us into Geulah, a world of complete peace and abundance, without war or suffering. The coming of Moshiach will complete Gd's purpose in creation - for us to make a dwelling place for Gd in this world by transforming and elevating the material things of this world into spirituality through learning Torah and doing mitzvahs and acts of goodness and kindness.

בס"ד

These Hebrew letters appear at the top of each coloring page.
This is an abbreviation for the Aramaic phrase "B'Sayata Di'shamaya,"
which means, "With the Help of Heaven."
This reminds us that everything comes from G-d.

ב״ה

On Purim
a big light
is revealed.
Purim is a day to be happy.

Happy Purim

בס"ד

THERE IS NOTHING
IN THIS WORLD
THAT'S NATURAL.
EVERYTHING
LOOK AND
SEE ALL OF
IS THE MIRACLES IN
YOUR OWN LIFE!
MIRACLES!

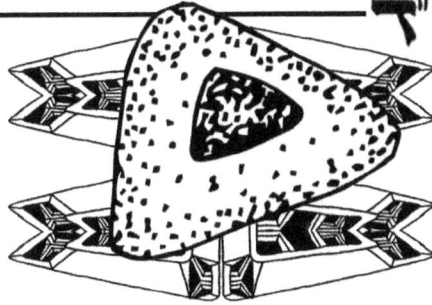

Purim is a day to be happy.

FORGET ABOUT YOUR PHYSICAL PROBLEMS, YOUR MATERIAL PROBLEMS, EVEN YOUR SPIRITUAL PROBLEMS. FORGETTING YOUR PROBLEMS ON PURIM DOESN'T MEAN GETTING DRUNK AND IGNORING YOUR PROBLEMS, HOPING THEY WILL GO AWAY. IT MEANS:

Knowing that G‑d is everywhere and also in your life.

WHEN YOUR RELATIONSHIP WITH G‑D IS STRONG, ALL OF YOUR PROBLEMS ARE SOLVED!

RABBI CHAIM Z. CITRON

Don't tell G‑d how big your problems are. Tell your problems how big G‑d is.

UNKNOWN

Happy Purim
from

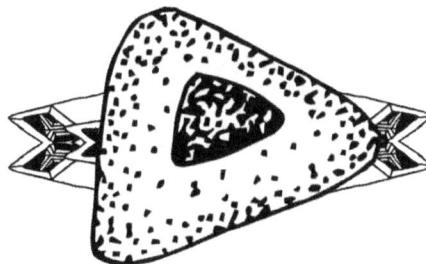

בס"ד

The days of Purim will last forever.

WHEN SHABBOS COMES, WHEN YOM TOV COMES, THE WHOLE WORLD IS A LITTLE BIT ELEVATED. THE SPARKS OF HOLINESS WITHIN US SHINE A LITTLE BIT BRIGHTER. EVERY SPARK IS AWAKENED AND ELEVATED WITH A LOVE AND DESIRE TO COME CLOSER TO G‑D AND THIS DESIRE HAS THE POWER TO PUSH AWAY THOSE THINGS THAT OBSTRUCT THIS CLOSENESS.

WHAT IS THE GOLDEN SCEPTER? G‑D'S INFINITE LIGHT TOUCHING THE WORLD, THE LIFE OF ALL THE WORLDS.

In front of G‑d there is no world

"I AM G‑D. I HAVE NOT CHANGED." THE WORLD CHANGES, BUT G‑D DOES NOT CHANGE. THE WORLD IS A FINITE CREATION OF THE INFINITE CREATOR.

To meditate on the Greatness of G‑d

HE FILLS THE WORLD AND SURROUNDS THE WORLD.

בס"ד

ENCLOTHED IN THE DAILY THINGS WE DO IS A GREAT MIRACLE.

PURIM IS A DAY WHEN EVERY THING IS TURNED AROUND. TURN EVERY THING THAT IS NEGATIVE IN YOUR LIFE INTO THE POSITIVE.

Holy Sparks

בס"ד

Purim celebrates
the unity of the
Jewish people and
our total acceptance
of the Torah, of our
own free will.

DO SOMETHING SINCERE FOR G-d.

When you send
shalach manos,
it is better to send
something small
from the heart,
than a big, fancy
basket without
sincere warmth.

ב"ד

When we do G‑d's will, G‑d neither slumbers nor sleeps.

THE MIRACLE OF PURIM WAS ENCLOTHED IN NATURE, G‑D'S NAME IS NOT EVEN MENTIONED ONCE IN THE MEGILLAH.
SUCH A HIGH LEVEL OF G‑DLINESS CAME SO LOW, IT PERMEATED THE PHYSICAL WORLD, AND LOOKED LIKE NATURE.

The way we behave to G‑d is how G‑d behaves to us.

Darkness to Light; Bitter to Sweet.

The King couldn't sleep.

THE PINTELE YID, THE G‑DLY SPARK IN EVERY JEW AWAKENS AND RISES.

G‑D
TORAH
MITZVAHS

WHEN A PERSON IS AWAKE, ALL OF HIS POWERS ARE REVEALED, BUT WHEN HE IS ASLEEP, HIS POWERS ARE CONCEALED. WHEN A PERSON DREAMS, OPPOSITES CAN BE CONNECTED BECAUSE THE INTELLECT IS ASLEEP.
THE POWER OF DISTINCTION IS ASLEEP, SO THINGS CAN GET MIXED UP.

The King of Kings "sleeps" when we choose not to do the right thing.

WHAT DOES IT MEAN THAT G‑D "SLEEPS?"
THE ORDER OF THE G‑DLY POWERS THAT DESCEND TO THIS WORLD CHANGES. THINGS THAT ARE HIGH LOSE THEIR POWERS AND THINGS THAT ARE LOW GAIN POWER TO DO HARM.

HOW IS IT POSSIBLE THAT WE, WHO ARE CONNECTED TO G‑D COULD POSSIBLY SIN? WHEN WE ARE PERMEATED WITH AWE OF THE KING, WE CANNOT DO WRONG. BUT SOMETIMES WE FALL ASLEEP, AND GO A LITTLE CRAZY. ONLY WHEN WE ARE CRAZY CAN WE SIN.

Torah and mitzvahs keep us in order.

Holy Sparks

Rabbi Y.Y.Shagalov PURIM MAAMER 5746

WWW.HOLYSPARKS.COM
©1990-2016 Rae Shagalov

בס"ד

½

The highest level is connecting our will to the King's will.

בס"ד

G*d is Always with us and always involved.

As one person; As one heart.

How?
By setting aside our external differences and recognizing the Divine Spark that is the essence of all of us.

TO THE DEGREE THAT WE ARE UNITED IS THE DEGREE THAT WE CAN RECEIVE THE TORAH.

Connect to the deepest place within you.

From scattering to gathering

The Torah is the vessel of oneness; Torah requires unity.

To be unified we have to touch our Essence, our G☆dly Essence.

Go beyond your personality.

Discover your inner essence.

Purim celebrates the unity of the Jewish people and our total acceptance of the Torah of our own free will.

ME, AS I AM, IN ALL MY DETAILS I'M UNITED WITH EVERY OTHER JEW IN ALL OF THEIR DETAILS, AND THEIR DETAILS ARE AS IMPORTANT TO ME AS MY OWN DETAILS.

THE JEW IN YOU IS THE EXACT SAME JEW AS THE JEW IN ANOTHER JEW.

Jews are Jews.

FROM THE HIGHEST TO THE LOWEST; NO JEW IS MORE JEWISH THAN ANY OTHER.

BE HAPPY ❀ IT'S ADAR ❀ ב"ה

SOMETIMES WE KNOW IN THIS WORLD

DID YOU THINK ABOUT HASHEM TODAY? DID YOU SMILE TO HASHEM TODAY?

SOMETIMES WE KNOW IN THE NEXT WORLD

TAKE ADVANTAGE OF PURIM! RISE EARLY SAY TEHILLIM DAVEN FOR ONE THING FOCUS ON ONE THING FOR 40 MINUTES.

ON PURIM

BE HAPPY

AND DAVEN TO HASHEM
THE KEDUSHA IS INCREDIBLE ON PURIM.
MAKE A LIST OF EVERYTHING YOU NEED
AND ASK FOR EVERYTHING
HASHEM LISTENS CLOSELY ON PURIM.

PURIM IS LIKE YOM KIPPUR. YOU CAN ACCOMPLISH SO MUCH SPIRITUALLY ON PURIM.

DON'T WASTE PURIM!
WAKE UP EARLY ❀ EXTRA EARLY!
AND SPEAK WITH HASHEM
EVERYTHING THAT IS ON YOUR
HEART. DON'T BE AFRAID TO CRY.
LET THE TEARS RUN DOWN YOUR FACE.

NO MATTER HOW GLOOMY THINGS SEEM, EVERYTHING CAN TURN AROUND. PEOPLE WALK AROUND WITH SUCH A HEAVY HEART. EVERYBODY STRUGGLES. THE WAY TO LIGHTEN UP A HEAVY HEART IS TO **Talk To Hashem** YOUR TEARS ARE VERY PRECIOUS TO HASHEM.

Rabbi Tauber

בס"ד

It's
Adar בָּה
Be Happy

The yetzer hara
hides and waits
in the one thing
we can't have!
IT'S ADAR!
BE HAPPY
WITH WHAT
YOU HAVE!
THANK THINK OF
       EVERY
G‑D   GOOD THING
FOR   IN YOUR LIFE!
EVERYTHING

ב"ה

Why does G‑d hide from us?

So that we will feel the pain of separation and return again.

Turn the pain into LIFE

Fill yourself with enthusiasm for life and you will be able to transform your pain.

Fill yourself with the love of G‑d and you will be able to overcome your difficulties.

Purim is a day to be Happy.

FORGET ABOUT YOUR PHYSICAL PROBLEMS, YOUR MATERIAL PROBLEMS, EVEN YOUR SPIRITUAL PROBLEMS.

IN ORDER TO SOLVE YOUR PROBLEMS, YOU HAVE TO TRANSCEND YOUR PROBLEMS. IN ORDER TO TRANSCEND YOUR PROBLEMS, YOU HAVE TO YIELD YOURSELF. YOU HAVE TO TRANSCEND YOURSELF.

There is a joy that comes with knowing that G‑d is everywhere and G‑d is also here.

FORGETTING YOUR PROBLEM ON PURIM DOESN'T MEAN GETTING DRUNK AND IGNORING YOUR PROBLEMS HOPING THEY WILL GO AWAY. IT MEANS KNOWING THAT G‑D IS EVERYWHERE AND ALSO IN YOUR LIFE. WHEN YOUR RELATIONSHIP WITH G‑D IS STRONG, ALL OF YOUR PROBLEMS ARE SOLVED

Rabbi Chaim Z. Citron
Purim Seudah 5760

בס״ד

NESS
HISTAR
HIDDEN
MIRACLE

THE MIRACLE IN
MEGILLAS ESTHER
IS COMPLETELY
HIDDEN. THE NAME
OF G‑D IS NOT
MENTIONED EVEN
ONCE.

SOMETIMES
THE PAIN
WE GO THROUGH
IS WHERE
THE MIRACLE
COMES OUT

בס"ד

CLARITY BRINGS
JOY **The Hidden Spark**

The whole Jewish people are called Esther.

THE G☺DLINESS IS HIDDEN IN THIS WORLD JUST AS G☺D WAS HIDDEN IN THE STORY OF ESTHER.

WHEN THE G☺DLY SPARK WITHIN US IS CONCEALED IN THE THOUGHTS SPEECH AND DEEDS OF THIS WORLD, IT IS LIKE A DOT IN THE CASTLE. THERE IS NO PERSON WHO DOES NOT HAVE THIS INWARDNESS, BUT EACH PERSON HAS A DIFFERENT WAY OF BRINGING IT OUT. THIS HIDDENNESS IS CALLED **Esther.**

Happy Purim.

Holy Sparks

Happy Purim

בס"ד

Holy Sparks www.HOLYSPARKS.COM ©1990-2016 Rae Shagalov

Happy Purim

בס"ד

DON'T WORRY.
DEPRESSED
YOU'RE
GOING TO BE
A LITTLE BIT
IN YOUR LIFE
ANYWAYS—
YOU MIGHT
AS WELL
PUMP A
LITTLE
SIMCHA
IN!

It's
Adar!
Be Happy

בס"ד

Happy Purim
from

בס"ד

Happy Purim
from

בס"ד

Happy Purim
from

Holy Sparks
WWW.HOLYSPARKS.COM
©1990-2015 Rae Shagalov

בס"ד

Happy Purim
from

Holy Sparks
WWW.HOLYSPARKS.COM
©1990-2015 Rae Shagalov

פורים
שמח

Happy
Purim

בס"ד

Happy Purim
from

בס"ד

Happy Purim
from

Happy Purim
from

Happy Purim
from

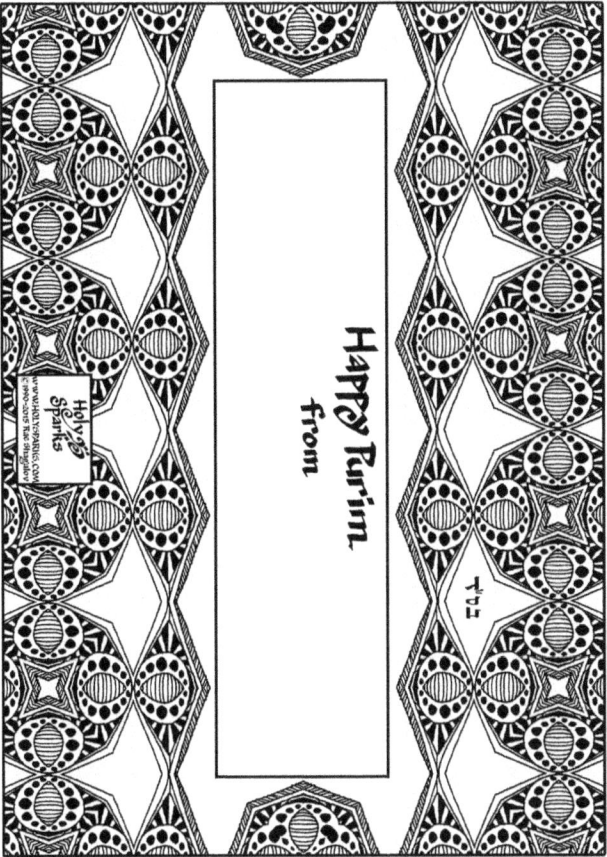

Happy Purim.
from

פורים

Holy Sparks
WWW.HOLYSPARKS.COM
©1990-2016 Rae Shagalov

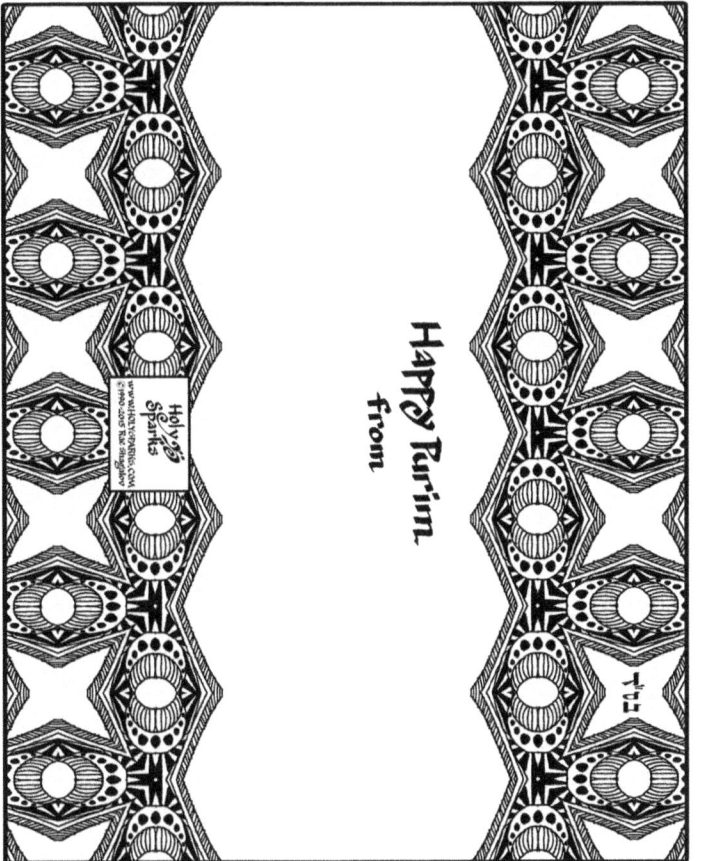

Happy Purim.
from

פורים

Holy Sparks
WWW.HOLYSPARKS.COM
©1990-2016 Rae Shagalov

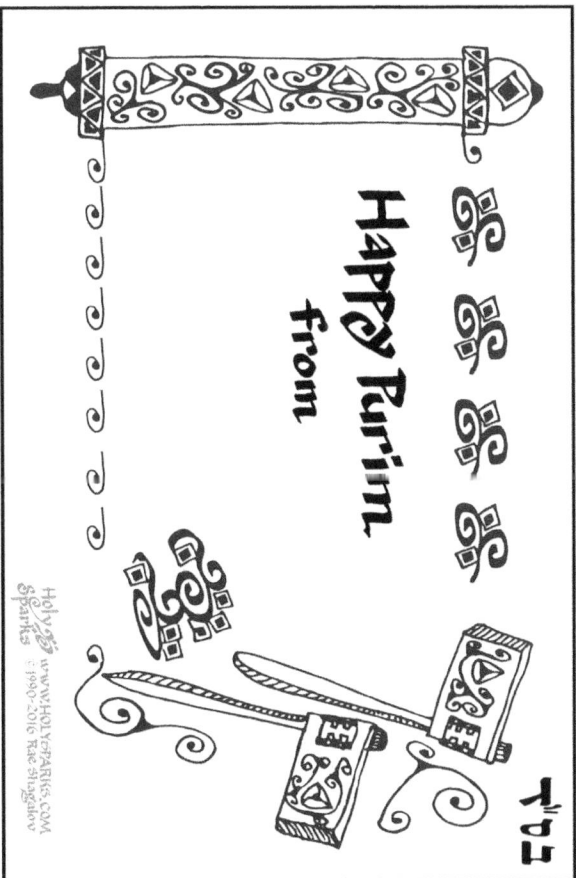

Happy Purim.
from

פורים

Holy Sparks
www.HOLYSPARKS.COM
©1990-2016 Rae Shagalov

Happy Purim.
from

פורים

Holy Sparks
www.HOLYSPARKS.COM
©1990-2016 Rae Shagalov

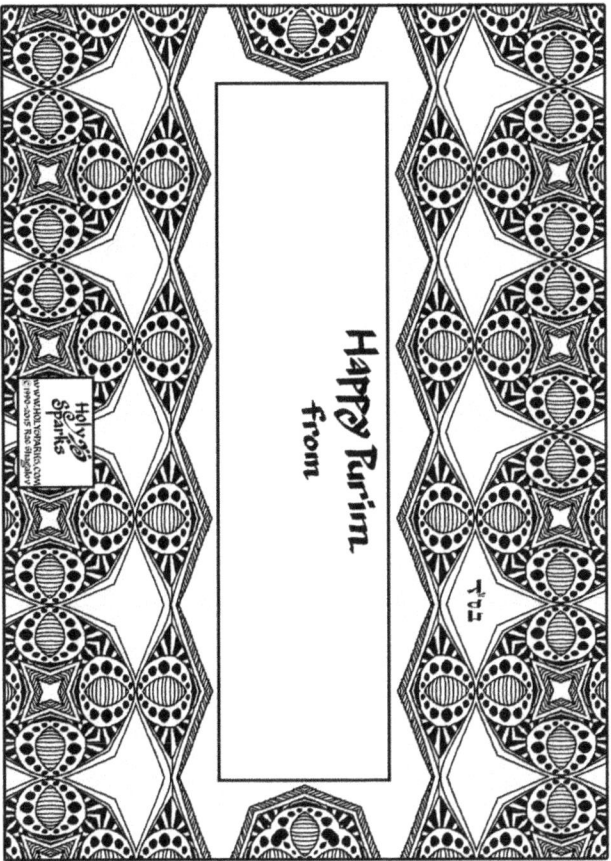

Happy Purim
from

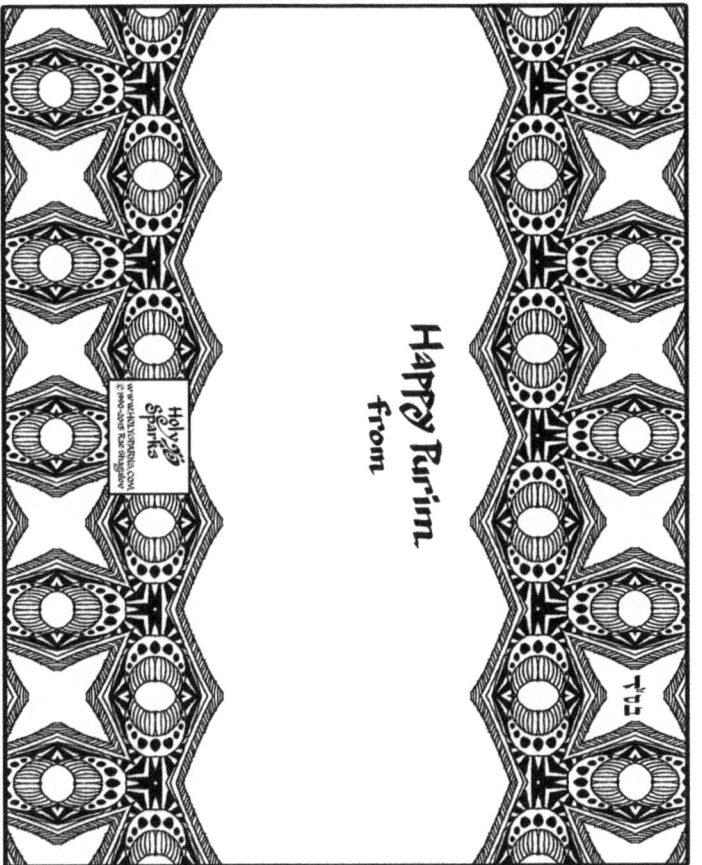

Happy Purim
from

Happy Purim
from

Happy Purim
from

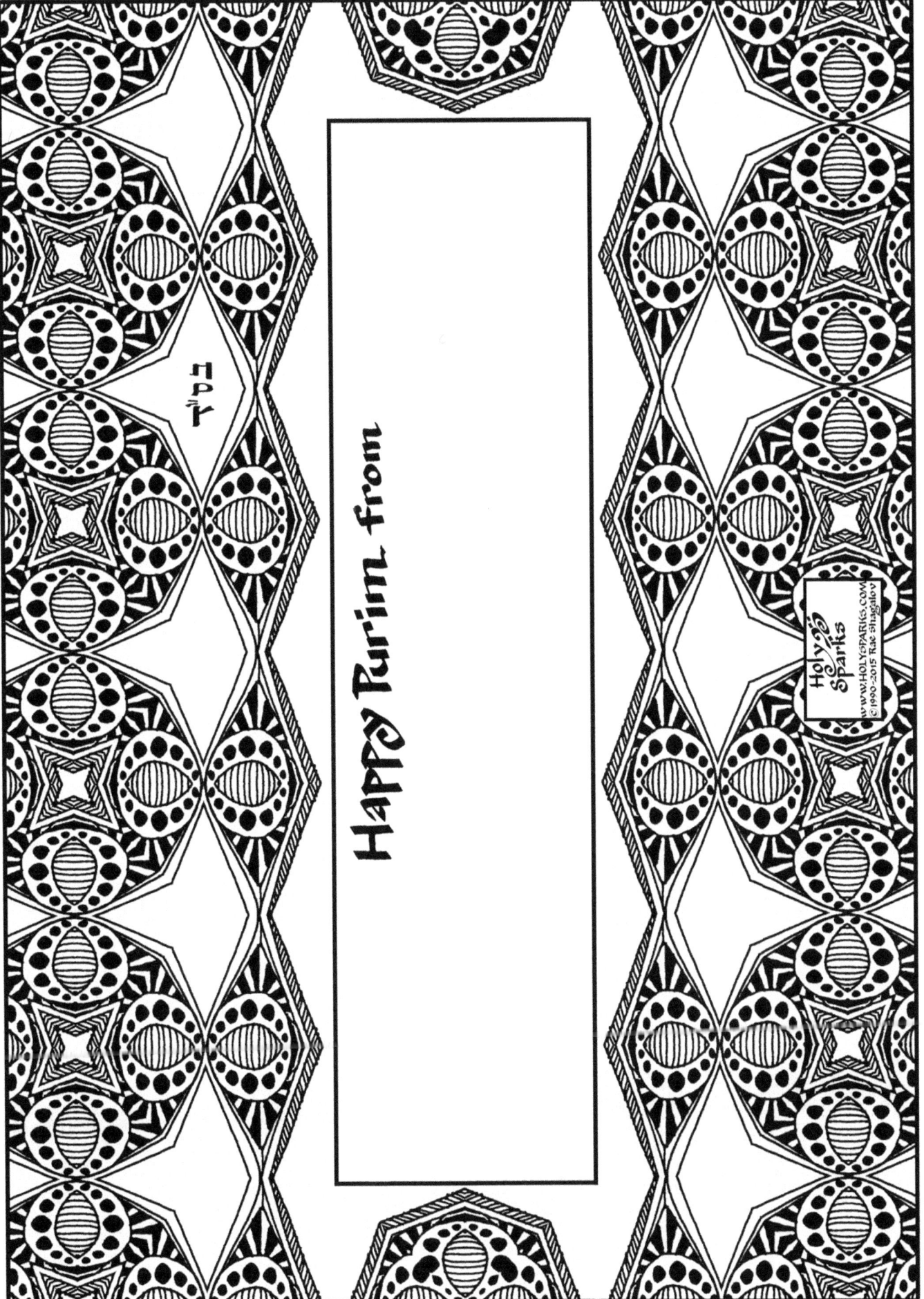

חג פורים

Happy Purim from

חג פורים

Happy Purim from

Happy Purim

Holy Sparks
WWW.HOLYSPARKS.COM
©1990-2015 Rae Shagalov

Happy Purim

Holy Sparks
WWW.HOLYSPARKS.COM
©1990-2015 Rae Shagalov

Happy Purim

Happy Purim

Happy Purim!

To be unified
we have to
Touch our
Essence,
our Godly
Essence.

There is nothing
in this world
that's natural.
EVERYTHING
look and
see all of
the miracles in
your own life!
IS
MIRACLES

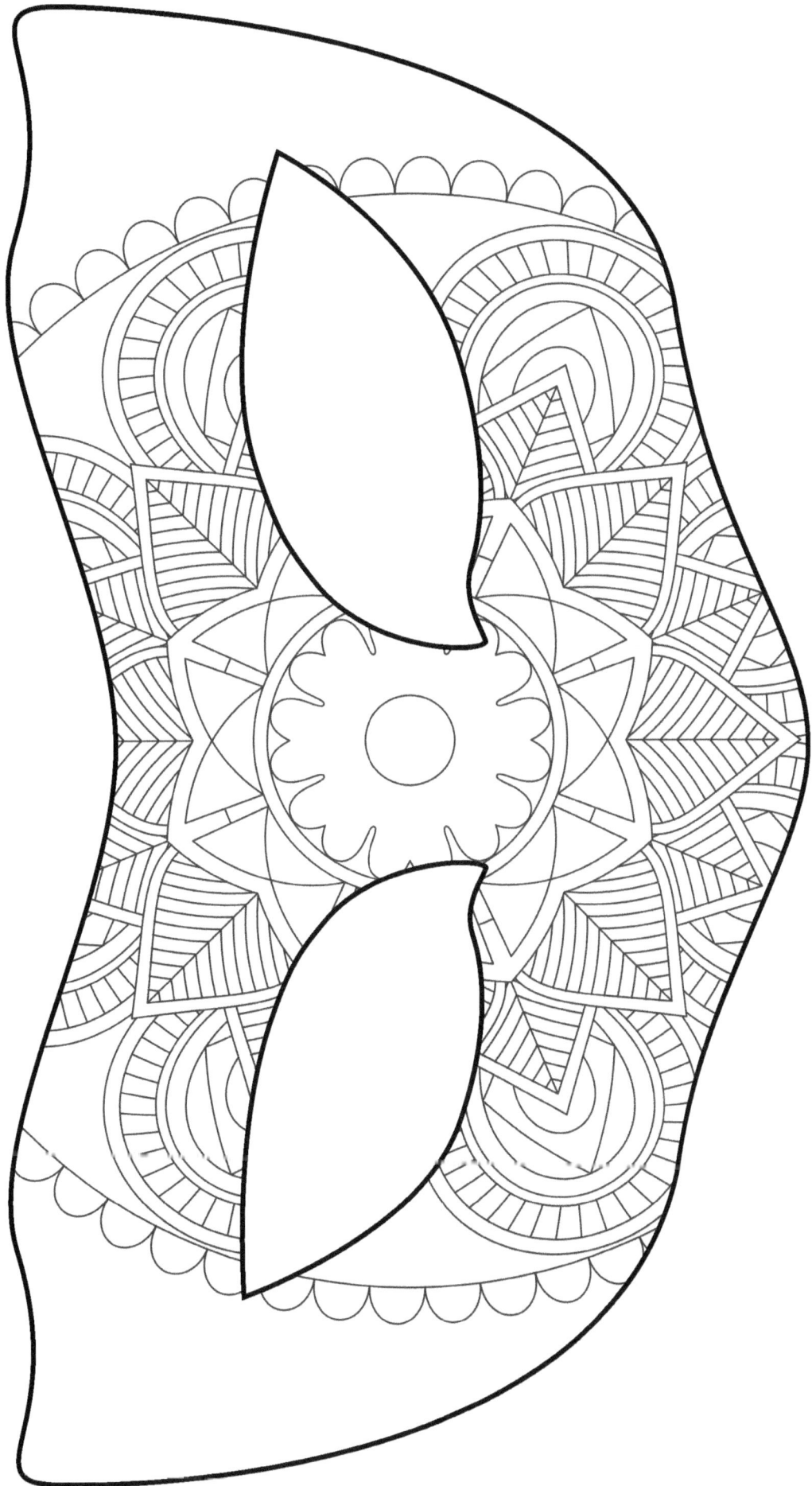

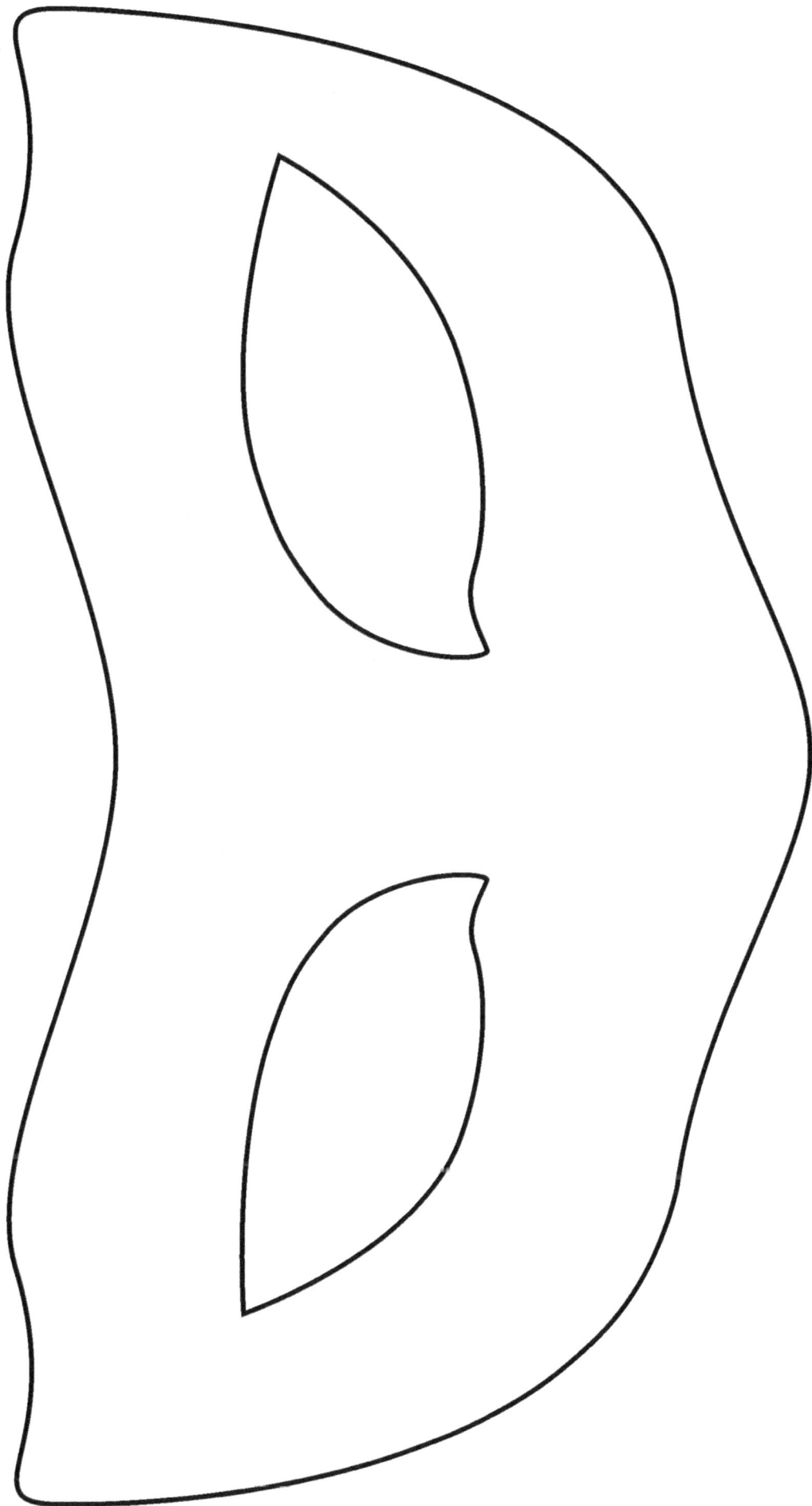

✌ 10 WAYS TO BE JOYFULLY JEWISH ✌

The most important principle in the Torah is the protection of Jewish life. It's more important than Shabbat, more important than holidays, even fasting on Yom Kippur. Right now, in Israel, and everywhere, Jews must stand together in unity and do whatever possible to protect Jewish life.

The Rebbe, Rabbi Menachem M. Schneerson of Lubavitch, teaches that there are ten important *Mitzvahs we can do to protect life. See what you can do:

1) AHAVAS YISROEL: Behave with love towards another Jew.
2) LEARN TORAH: Join a Torah class.
3) Make sure that Jewish children get a TORAH TRUE EDUCATION.
4) Affix kosher MEZUZAS on all doorways of the house.
5) For men and boys over 13: Put on TEFILLIN every weekday.
6) Give CHARITY.
7) Buy JEWISH HOLY BOOKS and learn them.
8) Light SHABBAT & YOM TOV CANDLES. A Mitzvah for women and girls.
9) Eat and drink only KOSHER FOOD.
10) Observe the laws of JEWISH FAMILY PURITY.

In addition the Rebbe urges that:

Every Jewish man, woman and child should have a letter written for them in a **Sefer Torah.

Every person should study either the Rambam's Yad Hachazakah -- Code of Jewish Law -- or the Sefer HaMitzvos.

Concerning Moshiach, the Rebbe stated, "The time for our redemption has arrived!" Everyone should prepare themselves for Moshiach's coming by doing random acts of goodness and kindness, and by studying about what the future redemption will be like. May we merit to see the fulfillment of the Rebbe's prophecy, Now!

----

*Mitzvahs are Divine Commandments that connect us to G-d.

**There are several Torah scrolls being written to unite Jewish people and protect Jewish life.

Letters for children can be purchased for only $1 via the Internet, at: http://www.kidstorah.org

Listen to inspiring Chassidic Torah classes while you color at Maayon.com.

For more information about how to be Joyfully Jewish, visit:

Holysparks.com   Moshiach.net   Chabad.org

Jewishwoman.org   Jewishkids.org   Maayon.com

Learn about the 7 special mitzvahs for Righteous Gentiles

Holysparks.com/pages/7-mitzvahs-for-non-jews

๛ Connect with Rae Shagalov ๛

Sign up to receive free art, coloring pages and Rae's Soul Tips newsletter! Go to: www.holysparks.com

Let's Connect!_

Facebook.com/soultips

Pinterest.com/holysparks

Twitter.com/holysparks

Youtube.com/holysparksbooks

Instagram.com/holysparks

๛ About Holy Sparks ๛

Holy Sparks is dedicated to spreading the light of authentic Jewish spirituality and wisdom. Holy Sparks provides and promotes Jewish knowledge, awareness and practice as it applies to people of all faiths and nationalities, regardless of affiliation or background. Holy Sparks helps spiritual seekers, particularly the Jewish people, and others who are looking for inspiration and encouragement, to discover and fulfill their individual talents and potential for service to G-d and mankind, through increasing in acts of goodness, kindness, and holiness.

๛ About Rae Shagalov ๛

Master calligrapher, Rae Shagalov, is the author of the Amazon bestseller, "The Secret Art of Talking to G-d," and the forthcoming 30 book "Joyfully Jewish" series

Rae is eager to share the beauty and wisdom of Torah through her 3,000 pages of beautifully designed Artnotes that reveal the special message of this exciting time in Jewish History. Her books provide her readers with very practical, joy-based action steps for infusing authentic Jewish spirituality into their daily lives. Rae is also an innovative educator who develops the talents of children at Emek Hebrew Academy in Los Angeles. You can view Rae's Artnotes, animated videos, and read her art blog at: www.holysparks.com.

There's a Holy Spark in each of us
that's hidden very well;
when it's revealed, we make our world
a place where G-d can dwell.

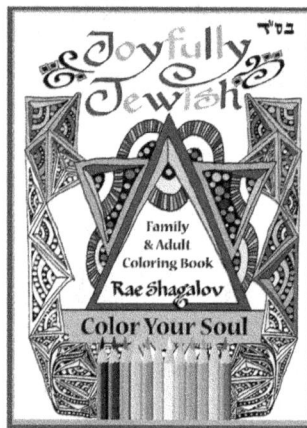

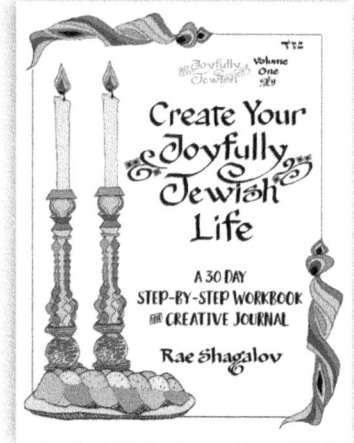